PEGASUS CHILDREN'S ENCYCLOPEDIA

UNIVERSE

CONTENTS

What is Universe? 3

Origin of the Universe 5

The composition of the Universe 8

Parts of the Universe 10

Black Holes, Pulsars and Quasars 17

Age of the Universe 23

Size of the Universe 24

Shape of the Universe 26

Evolution of life in the Universe 27

Ultimate fate of the Universe 29

Test Your Memory 31

Index 32

What is Universe?

The Universe is a huge wide-open space that holds everything from the smallest particle to the biggest galaxy. No one knows just how big the Universe is. Astronomers try to measure it all the time. They use a special instrument called a **spectroscope** to tell whether an object is moving away from Earth or towards the Earth. Based on the information from this instrument, scientists have learned that the Universe is still growing outwards in every direction.

Scientists believe that about 13.7 billion years ago, a powerful explosion called the **Big Bang** happened. This powerful explosion set the Universe into motion and this motion continues even today. Scientists are not yet sure if the motion will stop, change direction or keep going forever.

> Scientists believe that hydrogen comprises approximately 90 to 99 per cent of all matter in the Universe.

UNIVERSE

Many cultures have stories describing the origin of the world, which maybe roughly grouped into common types. In one type of story, the world is born from a world egg; such stories include the Finnish epic poem *Kalevala*, the Chinese story of Pangu or the Indian *Brahmanda Purana*. In the related stories, the creation idea is caused by a single entity emanating or producing something by himself or herself, as in the Tibetan Buddhism concept of Adi-Buddha, the ancient Greek story of Gaia (Mother Earth), the Aztec Goddess Coatlicue myth or the ancient Egyptian God Atum story. In another type of story, the world is created from the union of male and female deities, as in the Maori story of Rangi and Papa. In other stories, the Universe is created by crafting it from pre-existing materials, such as the corpse of a dead god — as from Tiamat in the Babylonian epic Enuma Elish or from the giant Ymir in Norse mythology. In other stories, the Universe emanates from fundamental principles, such as Brahman and Prakrti or the yin and yang of the Tao.

A space vehicle must move at a rate of 11 km per second to escape the Earth's gravitational pull.

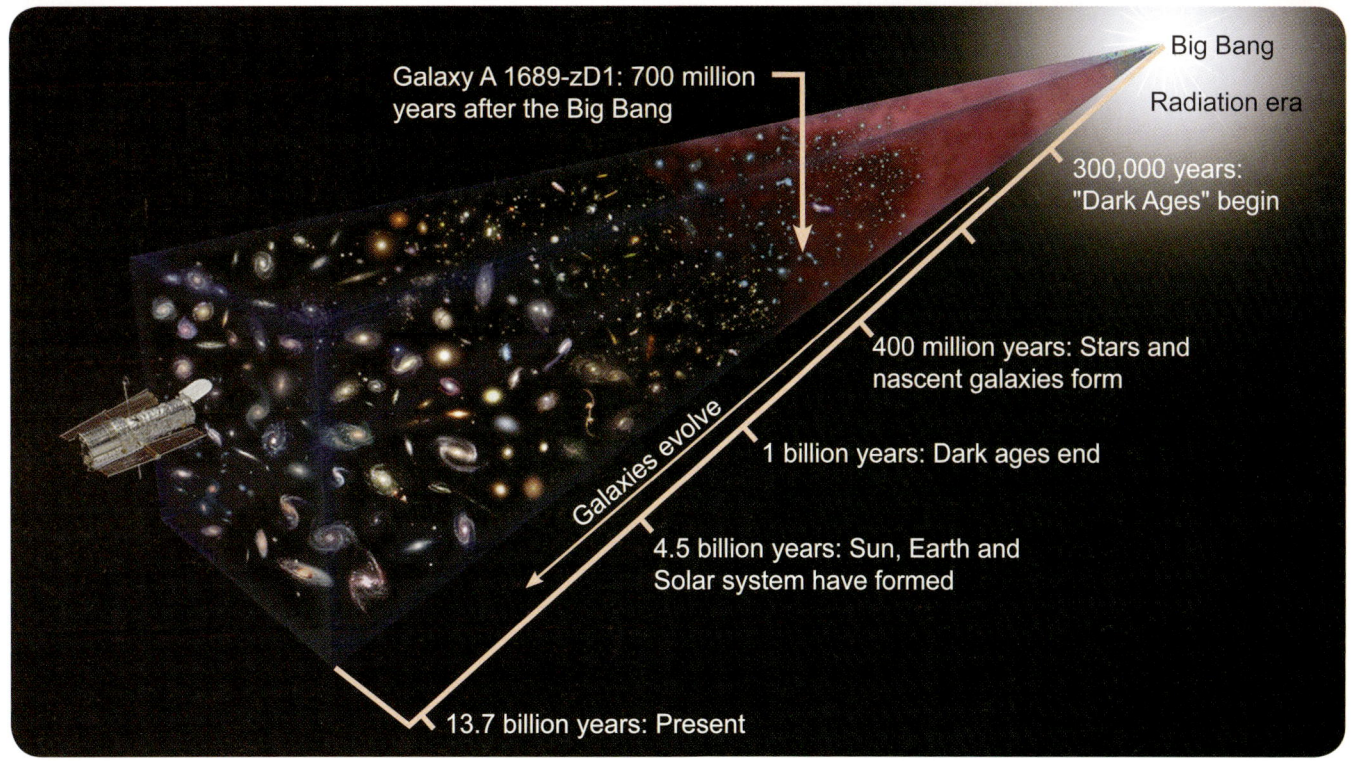

Origin of the Universe

Most astronomers believe that the Universe began in a Big Bang about 14 billion years ago. At that time, the entire Universe was inside a bubble that was thousands of times smaller than a pinhead. It was hotter and denser than anything we can imagine.

Then it suddenly exploded. The Universe that we know was born. Time, space and matter all began with the Big Bang. In a fraction of a second, the Universe grew from smaller than a single atom to bigger than a galaxy. And it kept on growing at a fantastic rate. It is still expanding.

As the Universe expanded and cooled, energy changed into particles of matter and antimatter. These two opposite types of particles largely destroyed each other. But some matter survived. More stable particles called **protons** and **neutrons** started to form when the Universe was one second old.

Over the next three minutes, the temperature dropped below 1 billion degrees Celsius. It was now cool enough for the protons and neutrons to come together, forming hydrogen and helium nuclei.

After 300000 years, the Universe had cooled to about 3000 degrees. Atomic nuclei could finally capture electrons to form atoms. The Universe was filled with clouds of hydrogen and helium gas.

UNIVERSE

The origin of the Big Bang theory can be credited to Edwin Hubble. Hubble made the observation that the Universe is continuously expanding. He discovered that a galaxie's velocity is proportional to its distance. Galaxies that are twice as far from us move twice as fast. Another consequence is that the Universe is expanding in every direction. This observation means that it has taken every galaxy the same amount of time to move from a common starting position to its current position. Just as the Big Bang provided for the foundation of the Universe, Hubble's observations provided for the foundation of the Big Bang theory.

Since the Big Bang, the Universe has been continuously expanding and, thus, there has been more and more distance between clusters of galaxies. This phenomenon of galaxies moving farther away from each other is known as the **red shift**. As light from distant galaxies approach Earth, there is an increase of space between Earth and the galaxy, which leads to wavelengths being stretched.

Halley's Comet is seen after every 76 years in the sky. It was last seen in the year 1986.

Origin of the Universe

In addition to the understanding of the velocity of galaxies emanating from a single point, there is further evidence for the Big Bang. In 1964, two astronomers, Arno Penzias and Robert Wilson, in an attempt to detect microwaves from outer space, inadvertently discovered a noise of extraterrestrial origin. The noise did not seem to emanate from one location but instead, it came from all directions at once. It became obvious that what they heard was radiation from the farthest reaches of the Universe which had been left over from the Big Bang. This discovery of the radioactive aftermath of the initial explosion lent much credence to the Big Bang theory.

The Big Bang theory provides a viable solution to one of the most pressing questions of all times. It is important to understand, however, that the theory itself is constantly being revised. As more observations are made and more research conducted, the Big Bang theory becomes more complete and our knowledge of the origins of the Universe becomes more substantial.

Astonishing fact

More than 75 million meteors enter the Earth's atmosphere everyday; but they disintegrate before hitting the ground.

7

The composition of the Universe

The chemical composition of the Universe and the physical nature of its constituent matter are topics that have occupied scientists for centuries. All over the Universe stars work as giant reprocessing plants taking light chemical elements and transforming them into heavier ones. The original composition of the Universe is studied in such fine detail because it is one of the keys to our understanding of processes in the very early Universe.

Human beings, the air we breathe, and the distant stars are all made up of protons, neutrons and electrons. Protons and neutrons are bound together into nuclei and atoms are nuclei surrounded by a full complement of electrons. Hydrogen is composed of one proton and one electron. Helium is composed of two protons, two neutrons and two electrons. Carbon is composed of six protons, six neutrons and six electrons. Heavier elements, such as iron, lead and uranium, contain even larger numbers of protons, neutrons and electrons. Astronomers like to call all material made up of protons, neutrons and electrons '**baryonic matter**'.

Until about thirty years ago, astronomers thought that the Universe was composed almost entirely of this 'baryonic matter', ordinary atoms. However, in the past few decades, there has been ever more evidence accumulating that suggests that there is something in the Universe that we cannot see, perhaps some new form of matter.

The composition of the Universe

According to the latest observational evidence, ordinary matter, including stars, planets, dust and gas, only make up a tiny fraction of the Universe (5 per cent). The rest is the elusive dark matter (25 per cent) and dark energy (70 per cent).

Dark energy: A mysterious (and as yet hypothetical) form of energy which is spread out uniformly throughout space (and time) and which has anti-gravitational properties. It is one of the possible explanations for the current accelerating rate of expansion of the Universe.

Dark matter: Matter not visible to us because it emits no radiation that we can observe, but it is detectable gravitationally.

Hydrogen & Helium gas: Hydrogen and Helium are the most abundant element in the Universe. This element is found in great abundance in stars and gas giant planets.

Astonishing fact

Saturn's rings are not solid. Although they appear to be thin, Saturn's rings are actually particles of ice, dust and rock. The particles range from the size of a grain of sand to larger than skyscraper buildings!

Stars: A ball of mostly hydrogen and helium gas that shines extremely brightly. Our sun is a star.

Neutrinos: A small particle that has no charge and is thought to have very little mass. Neutrinos are created in energetic collisions between nuclear particles. The Universe is filled with them but they rarely collide with anything.

Heavy elements: Planets like ours.

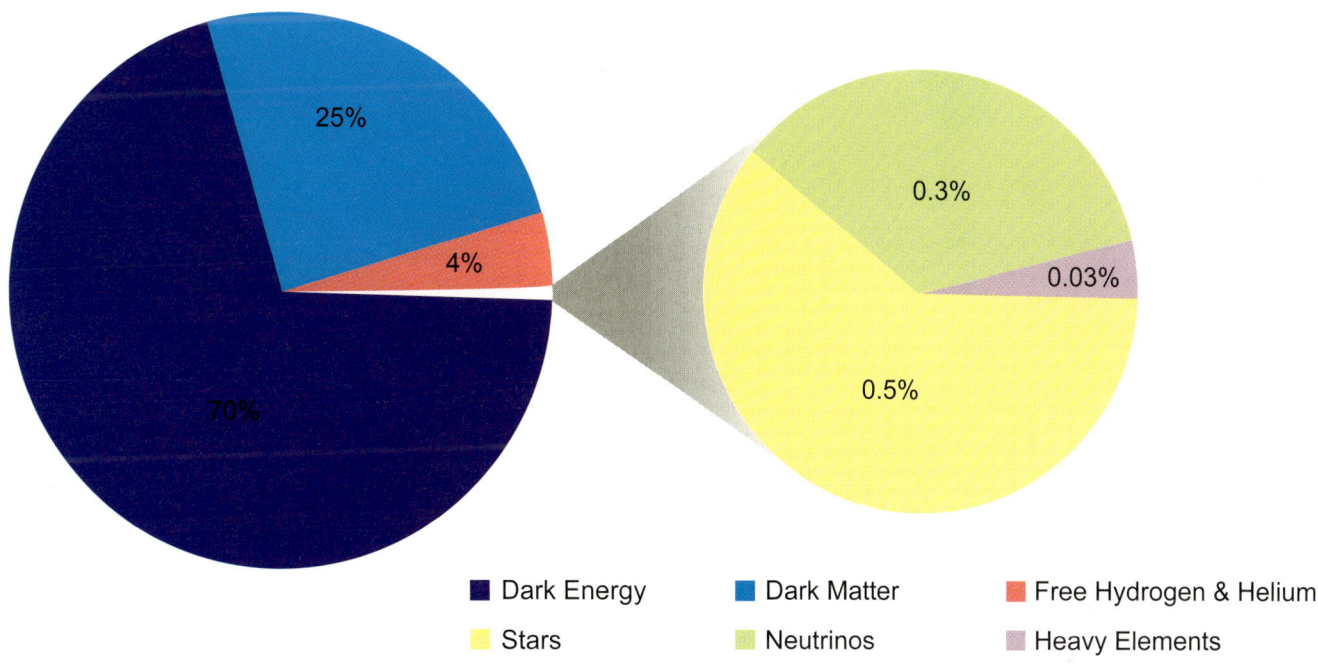

- Dark Energy
- Dark Matter
- Free Hydrogen & Helium
- Stars
- Neutrinos
- Heavy Elements

Parts of the Universe

Universe is the vast empty space around us and everything that is in it. It contains numerous heavenly bodies like the sun, the planets, moon, stars, meteors and meteorites.

The main constituents of the Universe are:

The solar system, the stars and the galaxies

The Solar System

The solar system consists of the sun, the nine planets and their satellites, asteroids, comets and meteors.

Sun

The sun is a huge, glowing ball at the centre of our solar system. The sun provides light, heat, and other energy to Earth. The sun is made up entirely of gas. Most of it is a type of gas that is sensitive to magnetism. Nine planets and their moons, tens of thousands of asteroids and trillions of comets revolve around the sun. The sun and all these objects are in the solar system. Earth travels around the sun at an average distance of about 149,600,000 km from it.

Astonishing fact

There are approximately 10,000 pieces of equipment revolving around the Earth. About 3,000 of these pieces are satellites, the rest are odd bits of debris.

Parts of the Universe

Planets

Our solar system consists of the sun, eight planets, moons, many dwarf planets (or plutoids), an asteroid belt, comets, meteors, and others. The sun is the centre of our solar system; the planets, their moons, a belt of asteroids, comets and other rocks and gas orbit the sun.

The eight planets that orbit the sun are (in order from the sun): Mercury, Venus, Earth, Mars, Jupiter, Saturn, Uranus, Neptune. Another large body is Pluto, now classified as a dwarf planet or plutoid. A belt of asteroids (minor planets made of rock and metal) lies between Mars and Jupiter. These objects all orbit the sun in roughly circular orbits that lie in the same plane, the ecliptic.

Astonishing fact

There are more stars in the Universe than there are grains of sand on Earth!

The largest planet is Jupiter. It is followed by Saturn, Uranus, Neptune, Earth, Venus, Mars, Mercury, and finally, tiny Pluto (the largest of the dwarf planets). Jupiter is so big that all the other planets could fit inside it.

The planets do not have light of their own. They appear brighter when light from the sun falls on them. The surface of the planet reflects the sunlight due to which the planet shines.

UNIVERSE

Natural satellites

An object which revolves round a planet (as the moon revolves around the Earth) is called a **satellite**. The word comes from the Latin word 'satellites', meaning 'attendant'. All satellites move round their parent planets in paths called **orbits**. Seven out of the nine planets in the solar system have satellites or moons. The only two planets which do not have satellites or moon are Mercury and Venus. The Earth has only one moon. The moon of the Earth completes one revolution around the Earth is 27.3 days. It also takes 27.3 days to complete on rotation on its axis. The moon is much smaller than the Earth.

Comets

These are heavenly objects which revolve round the sun like planets but have a very long period of revolution. A comet has a distinct head and a glowing tail which is always directed away from the sun. It brightens as it approaches the sun. Once in many years one happens to see a comet with the naked eye.

Astonishing fact

The sun travels around the galaxy once every 200 million years—a journey of 100,000 light years.

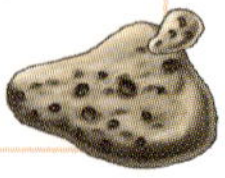

Parts of the Universe

Astonishing fact
Did you know that if you fell into a black hole, you would stretch like spaghetti!

Meteors and meteorites

Meteors are small heavenly objects moving round the sun. Sometimes, they get displaced from their orbit and enter the Earth's atmosphere from outer space with a very high speed. Friction between these objects and atmospheric air causes the objects to get red hot and finally burn out. Meteors are seen as bright streaks of light in the sky. They are therefore called **shooting stars**.

Sometimes, meteors of greater size reach the Earth without getting burnt. Then these are called **meteorites**. Some of the meteorites can be seen in museums.

Asteroids

Asteroids are small heavenly bodies that lie between the orbits of Mars and Jupiter. These are much smaller than a planet and orbit round the sun.

UNIVERSE

Astonishing fact

The nearest galaxy to Earth is Sagittarius Dwarf. It was discovered in 1954 with a distance of 82 light years away followed by Large Magellanic Cloud.

Stars

Each **star** in the sky is an enormous glowing ball of gas. Our sun is a medium-sized star. Stars can live for billions of years. A star is born when an enormous cloud of hydrogen gas collapses until it is hot enough to burn nuclear fuel (producing tremendous amounts heat and radiation). As the nuclear fuel runs out (in about 5 billion years), the star expands and the core contracts, becoming a giant star which eventually explodes and turns into a dim, cool object (a black dwarf, neutron star or black hole, depending on its initial mass). The largest stars have the shortest life span (still billions of years); more massive stars burn hotter and faster than their smaller counterparts (like the sun).

Stars twinkle due to air currents in the atmosphere. The colour of any star depends upon its temperature. They appear to be near each other, but actually they are apart by distances of billions of kilometres. These distances are measured in terms of a very big unit of distance called **light year**. Light year is used to measure distances in the Universe. One light year is the distance travelled by light in one year.

Parts of the Universe

Galaxy

A **Galaxy** or nebula is any large-scale system of stars, interstellar gas, dust and plasma within the Universe. Galaxies have different shapes and sizes. Our galaxy is called the **Milky Way**. This galaxy is spiral in shape and is wider at the centre. It appears as a huge strip of faintly glowing light from north is south across the sky. The sun and about 20 billion stars are a part of this galaxy. There are around hundred billion galaxies in the Universe. These galaxies are the building blocks of the Universe as atoms are the building units of the all substances.

Astonishing fact

The Milky Way galaxy is whirling rapidly, spinning our sun and all its other stars at around 100 million km per hour!

Constellations

A **constellation** is a group of stars which when seen from Earth, form a pattern. The stars in the sky are divided into 88 constellations.

The brightest constellation is **Crux** (the Southern Cross). The constellation with the greatest number of visible stars in it is **Centaurus** (the Centaur - with 101 stars). The largest constellation is **Hydra** (The Water Snake) which extends over 3.158 per cent of the sky.

UNIVERSE

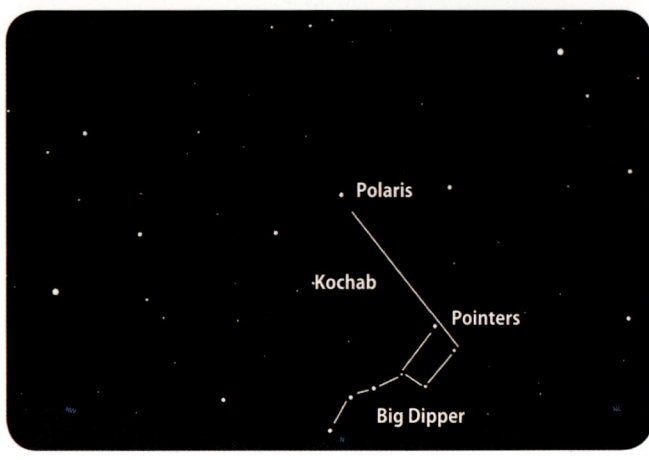

Pole Star

This is a star which is seen directly above the North Pole on the axis of rotation of the Earth. The term 'the Pole Star' usually refers to Polaris, which is the current northern pole star, also known as the **North Star**. It remains stationary at the same place in the north. It is not too bright and has no other star around it. All constellations appear to revolve around the Pole Star. The Pole star lies on the imaginary line joining the two stars, at the end of Ursa Major in the North direction. In ancient times, the Pole Star was used for navigation by the sailors at sea.

Artificial satellites

Artificial satellites are man-made vehicles launched by rockets into the orbit around the Earth. All the artificial satellites have a finite life and will eventually burn like meteors. Artificial satellites have a number of uses or functions. They maybe weather satellites, communication satellites or those which provide information about Earth's resources, etc. While the weather satellites help in forecasting weather conditions and provide warning of cyclones, communication satellites relay telephone and television signals, allowing live transmission of events from all parts of the world.

These artificial satellites can be observed as bright stars, travelling across the sky either just after sunset of before sunrise.

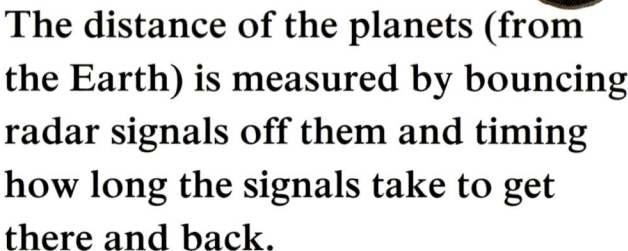

The distance of the planets (from the Earth) is measured by bouncing radar signals off them and timing how long the signals take to get there and back.

Black Holes, Pulsars and Quasars

Black Holes

A **black hole** is a region in space where gravitational force is so strong that nothing can escape from it. A black hole is invisible because it even traps light. The fundamental descriptions of black holes are based on equations in the theory of general relativity developed by the German-born physicist, Albert Einstein.

The gravitational force is strong near a black hole because all the black hole's matter is concentrated at a single point in its centre. Physicists call this point a singularity. It is believed to be much smaller than an atom's nucleus.

The surface of a black hole is known as the **event horizon**. This is not a normal surface that you could see or touch. At the event horizon, the pull of gravity becomes infinitely strong. Thus, an object can exist there for only an instant as it plunges inward at the speed of light!

Astonishing fact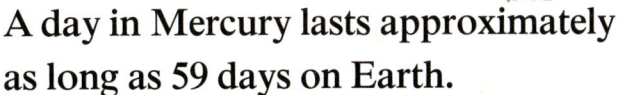

A day in Mercury lasts approximately as long as 59 days on Earth.

UNIVERSE

According to general relativity, a black hole can form when a massive star runs out of nuclear fuel and is crushed by its own gravitational force. While a star burns fuel, it creates an outward push that counters the inward pull of gravity. When no fuel remains, the star can no longer support its own weight. As a result, the core of the star collapses. If the mass of the core is three or more solar masses, the core collapses into a singularity in a fraction of a second.

As they are so small, distant and dark, black holes cannot be directly observed. Yet scientists have confirmed their long-held suspicions that they exist. This is typically done by measuring mass in a region of the sky and looking for areas of large, dark mass.

Many black holes exist in binary star systems. A binary star is a pair of stars that orbit each other. These holes may continually pull mass from their neighboring star, growing the black hole and shrinking the other star, until the black hole is large and the companion star has completely vanished.

Astonishing fact

The nearest star to us is Proxima Centauri with a distance of 39, 923, 310 million km or 4.22 light years followed by Alpha Centauri at 41, 531, 595 million km or 4.39 light years.

Pulsars

Pulsars are types of neutron stars. A neutron star is the highly compacted core of a dead star, left behind in a supernova explosion. What sets pulsars apart from regular neutron stars is that they are highly magnetized and rotating at enormous speeds. Astronomers detect them by the radio pulses they emit at regular intervals.

A pulsar is formed when a massive star collapses, exhausts its supply of fuel. It blasts out in a giant explosion known as a supernova, the most powerful and violent event in the Universe. Without the opposing force of nuclear fusion to balance it, gravity begins to pull the mass of the star inward until it implodes. In a pulsar, gravity compacts the mass of the star until it forms an object composed primarily of neutrons packed so tightly that they no longer exist as normal matter.

Astonishing fact

The brightest galaxy in the Universe is Large Magellanic Cloud with a distance of 0.17 million light years from Earth followed by Small Magellanic Cloud with a distance of 0.21 million light years from Earth.

UNIVERSE

Pulsars were discovered in 1967 by Anthony Hewish and Jocelyn Bell at the radio astronomy observatory at Cambridge. Pulsars are found mainly in the Milky Way, within about 500 light-years of the plane of the galaxy. A complete survey of the pulsars in the galaxy is impossible, as weak pulsars can only be detected if they are nearby. Radio surveys have now covered almost the whole sky, and over 300 pulsars have been located.

Pulsars are very strongly magnetised neutron stars, with fields of strength reaching 100 million Tesla (1 million million Gauss, compared with less than 1 Gauss for the Earth's magnetic field). The rapid rotation therefore makes them powerful electric generators, capable of accelerating charged particles to energies of a thousand million million Volts. These charged particles are, in some way as yet unknown, responsible for the beam of radiation in radio, light, X-rays and gamma rays. Their energy comes from the rotation of the star, which must therefore be slowing down. This slowing down can be detected as a lengthening of the pulse period. Typically a pulsar rotation rate slows down by one part in a million each year: the Crab Pulsar, which is the youngest and most energetic known, slows by one part in two thousand each year.

Astonishing fact

Hubble's law showed that Universe is getting bigger and so must have started very small. This led to the idea of Big Bang.

Black Holes, Pulsars and Quasars

Quasars

Many astronomers believe that quasars are the most distant objects detected in the Universe. Quasars give off enormous amounts of energy. They can be a trillion times brighter than the sun! Quasars are believed to produce their energy from massive black holes in the centre of the galaxies in which the quasars are located. Because quasars are so bright, they drown out the light from all the other stars in the same galaxy.

Despite their brightness, due to their great distance from Earth, no quasars can be seen with an unaided eye. Energy from quasars takes billions of years to reach the Earth's atmosphere. For this reason, the study of quasars can provide astronomers with information about the early stages of the Universe.

The word quasar is the short form for 'quasi-stellar radio source'. This name, which means 'star-like emitters of radio waves', was given in the 1960s when quasars were first detected. The name is retained today, even though astronomers now know most quasars are faint radio emitters. In addition to radio waves and visible light, quasars also emit ultraviolet rays, infrared waves, x-rays and gamma-rays. Most quasars are larger than our solar system.

Astonishing fact

During summer in Uranus, the sun does not set for 20 years. In winter, darkness lasts for 20 years. In autumn, the sun rises and sets every 9 hours!

UNIVERSE

Astonishing fact

There are about 100 billion galaxies in the Universe. The nearest spiral galaxy to our Milky Way is the Andromeda galaxy, which is 2.6 million light years away!

Quasars are the most distant objects to ever be detected in the Universe. They also have the largest red shift of any other objects in the cosmos. Astronomers are able to measure speed and distance of far away objects by measuring the spectrum of their light. If the colours of this spectrum are shifted toward the red, this means that the object is moving away from us. The greater the red shift, the farther the object and the faster it is moving. Since quasars have such a high red shift, they are extremely far away and are moving away from us at extremely high speeds. It is believed that some quasars maybe moving away from us at 240,000 km per second or nearly 80 per cent the speed of light.

The first identified quasar was called 3C 273 and was located in the constellation Virgo. It was discovered by T. Matthews and A. Sandage in 1960. It appeared to be associated with a 16th magnitude star like object. Three years later, in 1963, it was noticed that the object had an extremely high red shift. The true nature of this object became apparent when astronomers discovered that the intense energy was being produced in a relatively area. Today, quasars are identified primarily by their red shift. Today more than 2000 quasars have been identified.

Astonishing fact

Ceres is the biggest asteroid in the Solar System – 940 km across and 0.0002 per cent the size of the Earth.

Age of the Universe

The age of the Universe is defined as the largest possible value of proper time integrated along a time like curve from the Earth at the present epoch back to the Big Bang. The time that has elapsed on a hypothetical clock which has existed since the Big Bang and is now here on Earth will depend on the motion of the clock. According to the preceding definition, the age of the Universe is just the largest possible value of time having elapsed on such a clock.

It was estimated to be about 13.7 billion (13.7×10^9) years, with an uncertainty of 200 million years, by NASA's Wilkinson Microwave Anisotropy Probe project (WMAP). However this is based on the assumption that the underlying model that was used is correct. Other methods of estimating the age of the Universe give different ages.

Some recent studies found the carbon-nitrogen-oxygen cycle to be two times slower than previously believed, leading to the conclusion that the Universe must be at least 14.7 billion years old.

> **The Universe may have neither a centre nor an edge.**

Size of the Universe

The size of the Universe is 46 billion light years. This is the distance from planet Earth to the edge of the Universe. 1 light year is equal to 9.46 trillion km. The visible Universe has a diameter of 93 billion light years.

The observable Universe means the edge that light can travel. Remember that we see objects in the Universe because of light. The distance of these objects however, means light takes a long time to travel.

When we look at the Universe, we don't see it as it is, but as it appeared billions of years ago. When looking at faraway galaxies, the light reaching us have been traversing space for billions of years. For this reason, we see the objects and the Universe as it looked billions of years ago.

How does this relate to the size of the Universe? It allows scientists to calculate the dimensions. Scientists determine its size by (among other methods) multiplying the age via the speed of light (299,337 km per second). The age of the Universe is estimated to be 13.7 billion years.

The Virgo Cluster (cluster of galaxies) is 50 million light years away and is made up of 1000 galaxies.

Size of the Universe

Of course, these calculations are limited. It only accounts for the Universe which we can observe. The calculations for the dimension of the Universe go back only as far as light can reach. The rest of the Universe beyond light may well be much bigger.

Some make a distinction between the observable Universe and the actual physical Universe. The observable Universe is the 'edge', the farthest light can travel. Beyond that is the rest of space.

Calculating the size of the Universe can become even more complicated. The measurements don't take into account the expansion of the Universe. Today a lot of scientists believe the Universe is expanding. If that is the case, it means the Universe is getting bigger.

For example, the galaxy that was 2 billion light years away is moving farther away. It means light has to travel much farther to reach Earth. This will affect the calculations of the Universe's dimensions.

Light that travels 13 billion light years doesn't mean the galaxy is 13 billion years distant. With the expanding Universe, it could be much farther.

Astonishing fact

Halley predicted that a comet he had discovered would return in 1758, 16 years after his death, and it really did! It was the first time a comet's arrival had been predicted, and the comet was named after him as Halley's Comet.

25

Shape of the Universe

There's a continuing discussion among astronomers regarding the actual shape of the Universe. Right now, the most widely accepted model supports that of a flat Universe.

This has been confirmed through accurate measurements made by WMAP (Wilkinson Microwave Anisotropy Probe), a spacecraft that maps out the differences in temperature of the cosmic microwave background radiation (CMBR) across the entire sky. These results, which only have a 2 per cent margin of error, were released in 2008.

Before these seemingly conclusive findings were released, discussions revolved around three possible shapes—flat, closed, and open. To ascertain the actual shape, majority of astronomers were in agreement that they only needed to determine a few significant information about the Universe. One of them was its density.

They knew that if the density was found to be approximately equal to an accepted critical density, then the best prediction would be that of a flat Universe. If it was lower than the accepted value, then the best prediction would favour an open one. Finally if it was higher than the critical density, the prediction would favour a closed Universe.

Evolution of life in the Universe

The Universe began with an unimaginably enormous density and temperature. This immense primordial energy was the cauldron from where all life arose. Elementary particles were created and destroyed by the ultimate particle accelerator in the first moments of the Universe.

There was matter and there was antimatter. When they met, they annihilated each other and created light. Somehow, it seems that there was a tiny fraction more matter than antimatter, so when nature took its course, the Universe was left with some matter, no antimatter, and a tremendous amount of light. Today, there is more than a billion times more light than matter.

About 4.6 per cent of the mass and energy of the Universe is contained in atoms (protons and neutrons). All life is made from a portion of this 4.6 per cent.

Astonishing fact

Planets have magnetic field around them because of the liquid iron in their cores. As the planets rotate, so the iron swirls, generating electric currents that create the magnetic field.

We are carbon-based life forms. We breathe oxygen. Carbon and oxygen were not created in the Big Bang, but rather much later in stars. All of the carbon and oxygen in all living things are made in the nuclear fusion reactors that we call stars. The early stars were massive and short-lived. They consume their hydrogen, helium and lithium and produce heavier elements. When these stars die with a bang they spread the elements of life, carbon and oxygen, throughout the Universe. New stars condense and new planets form from these heavier elements. The stage is set for life to begin. Understanding when and how these events occur offer another window on the evolution of life in our Universe.

UNIVERSE

Life in the Solar System

Human beings are the only intelligent beings living in our Solar System. There's plenty of excitement, though, about finding micro-organisms elsewhere in our neighbourhood. Recent discoveries on Earth suggest that where there's organic (carbon-based) chemistry, water and an energy source, there's life; no matter what the conditions. As these essentials are commonplace in space, there's a good chance that life is too.

Living organisms have been found alive and well in environments on Earth so apparently hostile that the presence of life on other Solar System bodies seems quite feasible. Mars, the planet that most closely resembles Earth, and Europa, one of Jupiter's moons, both show evidence of water, and so are the focus of plans to look for life.

Did life arise independently on each body? If not, could it have been transferred from one to another? If so, was the common origin a 'seed' planted, perhaps, during collisions with comets, or interstellar dust? Crucial to answering these questions will be greater knowledge about the structure and composition of comets and interstellar dust. Saturn's moon, Titan, also shows promise of revealing the conditions needed for basic organic chemistry to evolve into the chemistry that eventually leads to life.

Astonishing fact

Earth's atmosphere is the only atmosphere discovered till date in which human can breathe.

28

Ultimate fate of the Universe

The ultimate fate of the Universe is a subject of study in the field of cosmology. Either the Universe will exist forever or it will cease to exist at some time. It is unknown which of these possibilities will hold true. It is also not known whether the Universe will continue to support life.

Ever since scientists proved the Big Bang to be the most plausible cosmological theory, and since it only focused more on how it might have all began, their attention started to shift to how the Universe would end. Thus, 4 theories Big Crunch, Big Freeze, Big Rip and Big Bounce have been suggested.

The **Big Crunch** predicts that, after having expanded to its maximum size, the Universe will finally collapse into itself to form the greatest black hole ever.

On the opposite side of the coin, the **Big Freeze** foretells of a Universe that will continue to stretch forever, distributing heat evenly in the process until none is left to be usable enough. Hence, it is also known as the Heat Death.

A more dramatic version of the Big Freeze is the **Big Rip**. In this scenario, the Universe's rate of expansion will increase substantially so that everything in it, down to the smallest atom, will be ripped apart.

Astonishing fact

With powerful telescopes, astronomers can see galaxies 2 billion light years away. This means we see them as they were when the only life forms in Earth were bacteria.

In a cyclic or oscillatory model of the Universe, there will be no end for matter and energy. But for us and the Universe that we know of, there will definitely be a conclusion. In an oscillatory model, the Big Bang and Big Crunch form a pair known as the Big Bounce. Essentially, such a Universe would simply expand and contract (or bounce) forever.

For astronomers to determine what the ultimate fate of the Universe should be, they would need to know certain information. Its density is supposedly one of the most telling.

You see, if its density is found to be less than the critical density, then only a Big Freeze or a Big Rip would be possible. On the other hand, if it is greater than the said critical value, then a Big Crunch or Big Bounce would most likely ensue.

Astonishing fact

The first living creature in space was the dog Laika on board Sputnik 2 in 1957. Sadly, she died when the spacecraft's oxygen supply ran out.

The most accurate measurements on the cosmic microwave background radiation (CMBR), which is also the most persuasive evidence of the Big Bang, shows a Universe having a density virtually equal to the critical density. The measurements also exhibit the characteristics of a flat Universe. Right now, it looks like all gathered data indicating that a Big Crunch or a Big Bounce is highly unlikely to occur.

SETI is the Search for Extraterrestrial Intelligence—the program that analyzes radio signals from space for signs of intelligent life.

Test Your MEMORY

1. What is the Universe?

2. Describe the origin of the Universe.

3. What is the Universe composed of?

4. Describe the parts of the Universe.

5. What is a Black Hole?

6. What is the Solar System?

7. What is the age of the Universe?

8. Describe the size of the Universe.

9. Describe the shape of the Universe.

10. Describe the evolution of life in the Universe.

11. Do you think life exists on any other planet besides Earth?

12. What do you think is the ultimate fate of the Universe?

Index

A

antimatter 5, 27
asteroids 10, 11, 13
atoms 5, 8, 15, 27

B

baryonic matter 8
Big Bang 3, 5, 6, 7, 20, 23, 27, 29, 30
Big Crunch 29, 30
Big Freeze 29, 30
black hole 13, 14, 17, 18, 29

C

Centaurus 15
comets 10, 11, 12, 28
constellation 15, 22

D

dark energy 9
dark matter 9

E

Edwin Hubble 6

G

galaxy 3, 5, 6, 12, 15, 19, 20, 21, 22, 25

H

helium 5, 9, 27
Hydra 15
hydrogen 3, 5, 8, 9, 14, 27

L

light year 14, 18, 19, 20, 22, 24, 29

M

matter 3, 5, 8, 9, 17, 19, 27, 28, 30
meteorites 10, 13
meteors 7, 10, 11, 13, 16
microwaves 7
Milky Way 15, 20, 22
moon 10, 12, 28

N

neutrinos 9
neutrons 5, 8, 19, 27
neutron star 14, 19

O

orbits 11, 12, 13

P

particles 5, 9, 20, 27
planets 9, 10, 11, 12, 16, 27
Pole star 16
protons 5, 8, 27
pulsars 2, 17, 19, 20

Q

quasars 21, 22

R

red shift 6, 22

S

satellite 12
shooting stars 13
solar system 5, 10, 11, 12, 21, 22, 28
spectroscope 3
star 9, 14, 16, 18, 19, 20, 21, 22
sun 9, 10, 11, 12, 13, 14, 15, 21